Wild Bird Giclees by Duckie

PUBLISHED BY DUCKIE AND THE
GRACKLE, 2016

Duckie and the Grackle Gallery and Jewelry
Design Studio

Lake Jackson, Texas
979 236-8153 / Grackle999@gmail.com

Duckie's Wild Bird Giclees are available in
several sizes - canvas and paper.

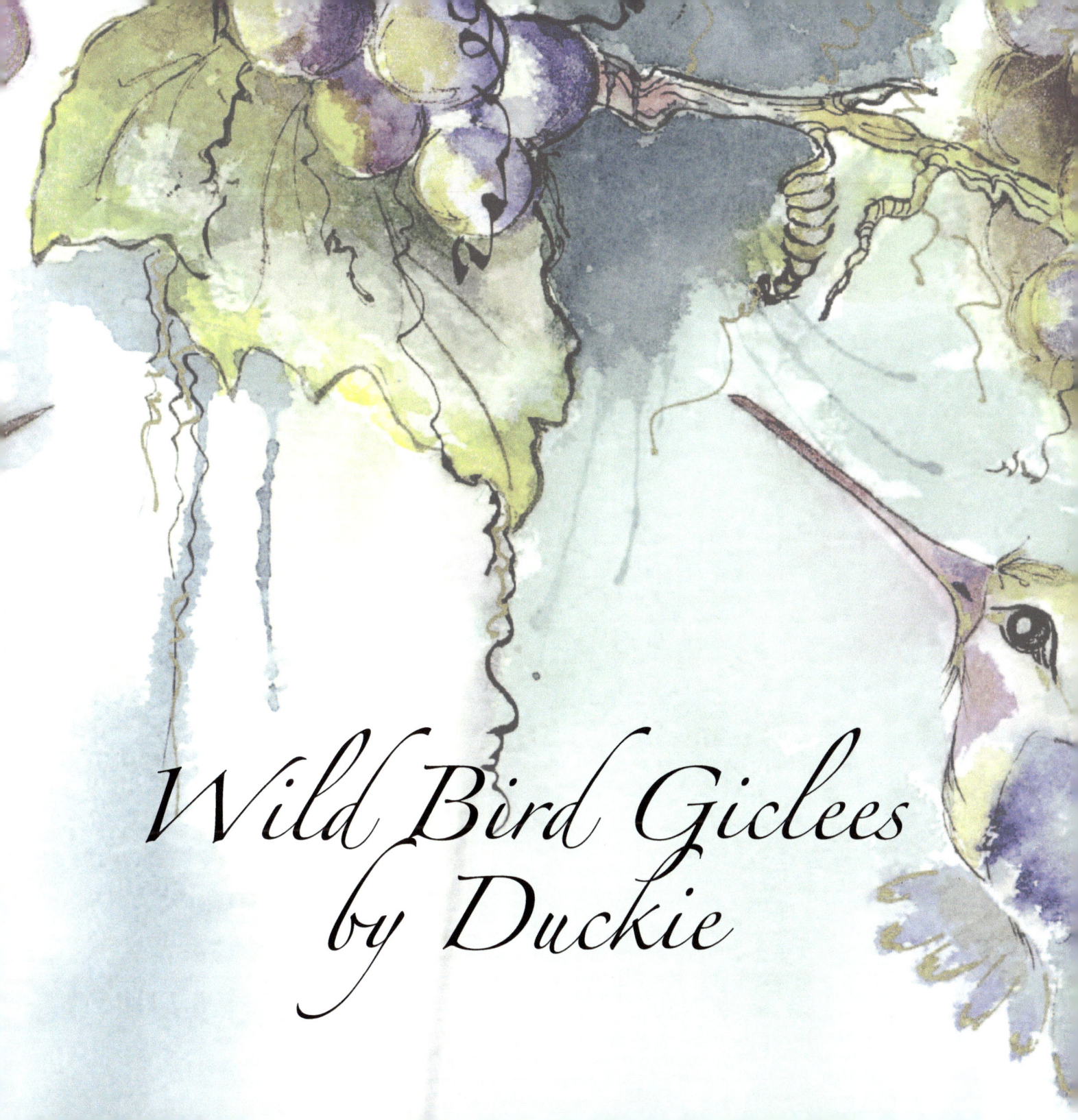

Wild Bird Giclees
by Duckie

This painting is the story of our "one day alive" cruise to the sludge islands just south of Port Isabelle. All these birds were there, including the mangrove warbler. Our quest was to find the mangrove warbler, a small bird that we are told is diminishing in numbers. He lives in the mangroves .

LAGUNA MADRE

- shore birds at Padre Island -

Look in the upper right hand corner, you'll find two to them there. The funny thing is that large birds such as the great blue heron were sitting in the bushes just poking their heads out to see what was going on. Wow! What an experience.

I painted these hummingbirds in grapes back in 2002 for my mother, Dickie Nowlin. She had taken a renewed interest in my painting and loved this piece.

MOM'S HUMMERS

hummingbirds

In 2011, we hung it in my jewelry studio at the gallery and began receiving wonderful comments, including offers to buy. So - here it is, fresh from the reproduction camera in Fort Collins, Colorado! I hope you love this piece as much as Mother did.

"FOR YOU, Dulcinea,
I mount the Stead of Spring
... riding a Daily Battlefield
... attacking Spinning Sky Sails
as knight errant
as fighter savant
... your warrior in red ...
for you, Dulcinea"

- Glenn Nelson McBride

This is Don Q IV, our magnificent warrior bird from the back patio. We can't tell for sure if he's won his mate's heart yet. He's sure been trying.

Don Quixote will live forever! The Grackle wrote his burning love song above.

FIGHTING CARDINAL

northern cardinal

This exotic pair of great blues were watched for several seasons by one of my customer couples. They live in the wetlands on the edge of Freeport, Texas - near Quintana.

If you continue down the highway past the wetlands, you will pass the Port of Freeport and continue over the big bridge onto Quintana Island.

Glenn and I observed the herons for several hours in morning and evening light. This is the light I experienced during the morning's "magic light," with the sun rising to light the shallows and then on to the Brazos River.

QUINTANA BLUE

- great blue herons -

South Texas receives hundreds of thousands of snow geese visitors each fall from the Arctic. We drive along fields of pure "snow." I was so inspired by my husband's music composition, *Flying*, that I just had to paint these geese leaving the cold North - heading for their Texas winter grounds.

From the great love song, *Flying*: "Turning! The sweet leaves are turning. A low sun is burning. We need to go there..."

A LOW SUN IS BURNING

- snow geese -

SPOONBILLS are the loveliest birds. My "Bill" is showing all his colorful brilliance, posed near a great blue heron. Grackle and I love to visit "Smith Oaks," across Galveston Bay … where hundreds of spoonbills gather to nest each Spring on a small lake. Clacking, clacking, clacking … they collide bills, steal sticks from each other … and entertain the tourists and photographers!
I love "Bill" and hope that you enjoy him in your room too!

- Duckie

BILL

- roseatte spoonbill & great blue heron

-

In 2007, I began studying
the young birds rescued by
Gulf Coast Wildlife Rescue.

Thanks to naturalist
Ed Barrios's incredible
photography, I brush-
painted these baby owls.
They posed for the world
right before their release
date back into the wild.
Maybe I'll see them again -
from a distance!

GIVE A TINY HOOT!

- baby owls

THE KISS

- wood ducks -

"come alive with me!
... come to the edge of the Pond
come alive with me
... and dance with me in love
come alive with me
... let's stay past the edge of Spring
"These beautiful wood ducks were presented on our first
Valentine's Day greeting card. I painted them from an exquisite
photograph by Michael Gray in 2011."

Talk about romantic!
Grackle and I were driving
through San Benard Refuge
near the Coast and couldn't
believe we were seeing
hundreds of hummingbirds
and dragonflies zooming
right along the ground. They
reminded me of fairies in
the grass! I love fairies in
the grass.
When we got back to
the studio, Grackle sat
and watched me paint -
mesmerized as always.
- Duckie

HUMMERS AND DRAGONFLIES

- hummingbirds and dragonflies -

THE FAIRIES IN MY GARDEN

- hummingbird and dragonfly -

Duckie loves hummingbirds and day lilies. She was happy to find them interacting in her backyard.
Just a few feet from her painting studio! Life is good.

RUNNERS OF THE ROAD AT HOME

- roadrunner family -

Roadrunners are one of my favorite birds. They stir up excitement wherever they're seen. Some of my customers have longtime roadrunner couples for friends. They will even bring "presents" to the back porch of the homeowner. Others will show up for some cat or dog food.
Those who see them with their chicks are really in for a treat!
- Duckie

CARRIE

- caracara -

Carrie is the female of a pair of crested caracaras. They live deep in the Brazoria National Wildlife Refuge less than 10 miles from my home. The *Master Naturalists* see her often and fairly close on the main refuge trail. The pair often sit on an observation tower roof when it's quiet.

Naturalist Ellis Burkhardt brought me an excellent close-up telephoto of Carrie's face. I hope you enjoy her as much as I do. She was our 2009 Print Collector's Calendar Cover Bird.

MEET ME IN A MERRY TREE

- cedar waxwings -

From a live sighting and field study. Every December, waxwings come through Brazosport, Texas. This group (and about 15 others) swept into the area like bandits. I watched them strip the neighbor's pyracantha bush of berries in a matter of minutes. Amazingly, waxwings sometimes pass berries between each other. It's something to watch!

... Meet me in a merry tree - a berry tree!

GOLDEN SLIPPERS

- snowy egret -

I have loved watching this "golden slippered bird" hunting early in the morning and late in the evening - feathers blowing in the Gulf breeze. He comes within a few blocks of my home.

Magic colors - sky, water sparkles, snow white feathers and gold!!

Our cardinals rule the courtyard at our home in Lake Jackson. We named the first pair "Don Q (for Don Quixote) and Dulcinea. Soon, we were naming our pottery glazes after the brilliant pair.

This spring, we're being entertained by Don Q, the Fourth (who is looking for his Dulcinea every day now!)

Redbirds are the most popular North American birds.

CARDINAL PAIR

- northern cardinals -

Black Skimmers love fishing along the Gulf Coast. At the mouth of the Brazos River, you can spot them skimming along with their flexible jawed beaks just below the water line.

They also love parking lots where I studied them over several days - flying, finding their own right tern and tending chicks!

SKIMMER PAIR

- black skimmers -

WHY CAN'T I BE LEADER?

- baby mockingbirds -

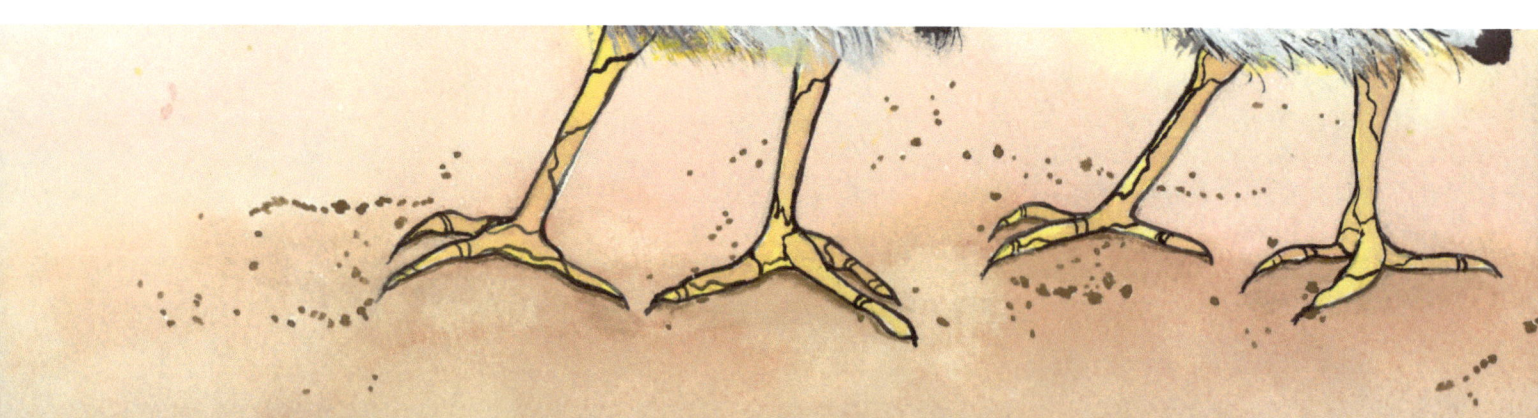

WELL, IT'S BETTER THAN A MUD CAVE!

- baby kingfishers -

"Baby Mockingbirds are
thick around our home
in Texas. They are real
characters and often tumble
out of their nests a little
early due to high breezes.
Usually, the parent will busy
around and rescue them.

After a windy night, I will
walk outside early and be
greeted by loud scolding,
viscious parents - just
daring me to pick up their
babies. They're tough on
cats too."

Painted from life.
- Duckie

WHY CAN'T I PLAY?

- baby mockingbirds -

Painted from a field study plus sketches and photos, I spent several hours with these baby herons. At this point, they are "fletched" and almost ready for flight. Like all feisty adolescents, they have become concerned about group position.

The crew had been rescued and were under the guard of *Gulf Coast Wildlife Rescue*. Sheree Etie was the wonderful heron expert and caregiver - and she lives gracefully on Little Slough with her beloved wildlife!

LITTLE SLOUGH BLUES

- baby great blue herons -

Painted during the incredible
morning light at Mustang
Island, Texas.

SILVER LIGHT

- great blue heron -

Painted during the evening
light at Mustang Island, Texas
- during a visit with our dear
friends, Milton Doolittle, Jim
Bob McMillan, Kathy and Bill
Mercer. The herons and the
golden late sky welcomed all of
us. It was a wonderful time.

GOLDEN LIGHT

- great blue herons -

Cardinals from our backyard!
Don Quixote and Dulcinea.

CARDINAL COUPLE PORTRAIT

- northen cardinals -

From a trip to Big Bend with Grackle, Milton and Jim Bob! Runners are the most delightful animals in the massive park.

- RUNNERS AT PANTHER JUNCTION -

- roadrunners -

Glenn and I captured some
incredible images of a yellow-
crowned night heron in love!
This was possible because
he was raised by Sheree Etie,
a heron expert in Brazoria
County. Although she tries
not to get entangled in lifetime
relations, Chickee Baby returns
every summer to Little Slough
to court her.

Here, he's moved up closer
to Sheree and is beginning to
display his courting feathers.
This is a sight seldom seen by
observers.
... From a series of paintings of
Chickee Baby - exquisitely in
love!

- CHICKEE BABY - DEUX

- yellow-crowned night heron -

At this moment, he's in full display for Sheree. This is one of a series of paintings of Chickee Baby - exquisitely in love! Painted from life.

CHICKEE BABY - TROIS

- yellow-crowned night heron -

Here, he's actually getting
ready to fly from Sheree to
a perch 30 feet away. This is
one of a series of paintings of
Chickee Baby - exquisitely in
love!-

CHICKEE BABY - QUATRE

- yellow-crowned night heron -

What a great thing to see your first flock of yellow-headed blackbirds! Grackle and I saw these birds feeding at a rest stop right north of Raton Pass! A flock of 30 or more bewildered us until I took this telephoto from the car window, catching them as they lifted off and over the vehicle.

This is an "exact reproduction" of the birds as they flew toward us. Lovely, lovely!!

WING MY DREAMS

- yellow-headed blackbirds -

It was a thrill to be selected as a Great Texas Birding Classic artist! These green herons were chosen as the 'poster birds' for 2009. This edition is printed with archival pigment inks onto the finest presentation paper. It should last through several generations of bird lovers.

HIDDEN TREASURES OF THE TRAIL

- green herons -

I painted this group of wading birds in my revised style of Melchior d'Hondecoeter, a 17th century Dutch bird painter (1636-1695). The Museum of Fine Art, Houston has one of his large pieces which Grackle and I visit often. No one has print-published it yet.

CHICKEE BABY EXPOSED

- yellow-crowned night heron, etc -

VISIT OR CALL Duckie at the largest wild bird art gallery on the Gulf Coast!
Giclees available on paper and canvas.
Duckie and the Grackle, 145 Oyster Creek Dr. STE 09, Lake Jackson, Texas 77566

979 236 8153
email: grackle999@gmail.com
DuckieandtheGrackle.com
DuckieandtheGrackle on facebook